D1205460

Awesome Ancient Animals

Sea Creatures Crawl on Land

Early Life

Dougal Dixon

An Hachette Company

First published in the United States by
New Forest Press, an imprint of Octopus Publishing Group Ltd

www.octopusbook.usa.com

Published by arrangement with Black Rabbit Books

PO Box 784, Mankato, MN 56002

Library of Congress Cataloging-in-Publication Data

Dixon, Dougal.
Sea Creatures Crawl on Land : Early Life / by Dougal Dixon.
p. cm. -- (Awesome Ancient Animals)
Summary: "Describes the animals of the Paleozoic Era, when
animals with bony parts and the first land animals developed.
Includes an Animal Families glossary, prehistory timeline, and
pronunciation guides"-- Provided by publisher.
Includes index.
ISBN 978-1-84898-626-8 (hardcover, library bound)
1. Paleontology--Paleozoic--Juvenile literature. 2. Animals, Fossil-
-Juvenile literature. I. Title.
QE725.D594 2013
560'.172--dc23
2012002747

Printed and bound in the USA

16 15 14 13 12 1 2 3 4 5

Publisher: Tim Cook Editor: Margaret Parrish Designer: Steve West

Contents

Introduction

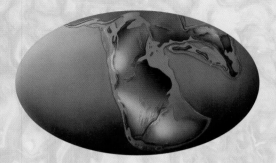

This map shows how the Earth looked at the end of the Paleozoic Era. Most of the Earth's continents are grouped into one mass of land.

This map shows how the Earth looks today. See how different it is! The continents have split up and moved around.

Awesome Ancient Animals follows the evolution of animals.

The Earth's history is divided into sections called eras, which are divided into periods. These last millions of years. *Sea Creatures Crawl on Land* takes you back to the Paleozoic Era, when animals with skeletons evolved and the first land animals and green plants appeared. We know about life in Paleozoic times because of fossils— plant and animal remains that have become hardened in rock.

A LOOK BACK IN TIME

This timeline shows how simple creatures evolved into many differnt and complex life-forms. This took millions and millions of years. In the chart, MYA stands for million years ago.

	BOOK	PERIOD	
CENOZOIC ERA	THE ICE AGE	1.81 MYA to now QUATERNARY	This is a time of Ice Ages and mammals. Our direct relatives, Homo sapiens, appear.
	ANCIENT MAMMALS	65 to 1.81 MYA TERTIARY	Giant mammals and huge, hunting birds rule. Our first human relatives start to evolve.
MESOZOIC ERA	CRETACEOUS LIFE	145 to 65 MYA CRETACEOUS	Huge dinosaurs evolve. They die out by the end of this period.
	JURASSIC LIFE	200 to 145 MYA JURASSIC	Large and small dinosaurs and flying creatures develop.
	TRIASSIC LIFE	250 to 200 MYA TRIASSIC	The "Age of Dinosaurs" begins. Early mammals live alongside them.
PALEOZOIC ERA	EARLY LIFE	299 to 250 MYA PERMIAN	Sail-backed reptiles start to appear.
		359 to 299 MYA CARBONIFEROUS	The first reptiles appear and tropical forests develop.
		416 to 359 MYA DEVONIAN	Bony fish evolve. Trees and insects come on the scene.
		444 to 416 MYA SILURIAN	Fish with jaws develop and sea animals start living on land.
		488 to 444 MYA ORDOVICIAN	Primitive fish, trilobites, shellfish, and plants evolve.
		542 to 488 MYA CAMBRIAN	First animals with skeletons appear.

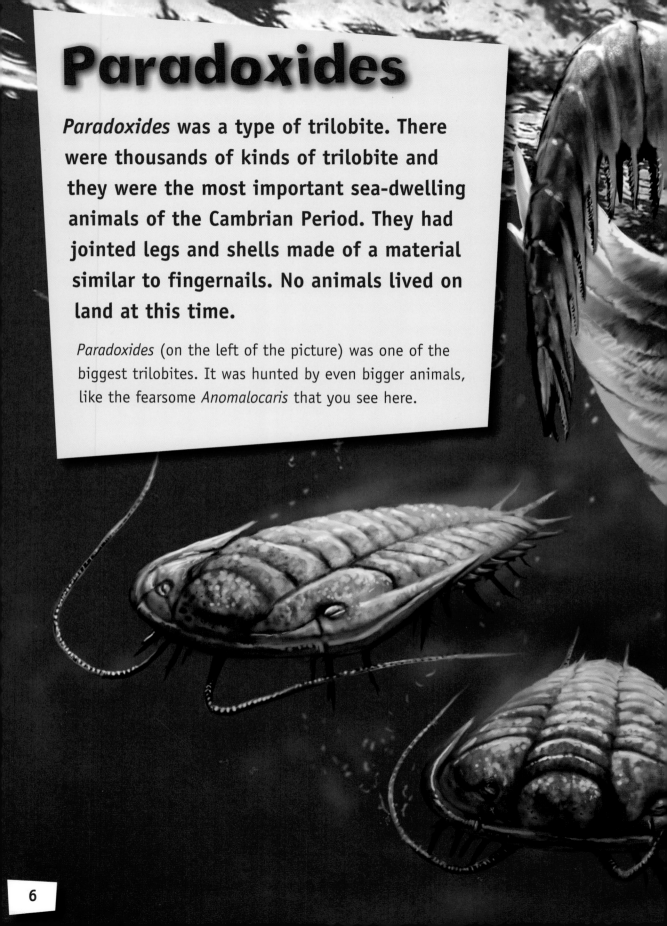

Paradoxides

Paradoxides was a type of trilobite. There were thousands of kinds of trilobite and they were the most important sea-dwelling animals of the Cambrian Period. They had jointed legs and shells made of a material similar to fingernails. No animals lived on land at this time.

Paradoxides (on the left of the picture) was one of the biggest trilobites. It was hunted by even bigger animals, like the fearsome *Anomalocaris* that you see here.

Animal fact file

NAME: PARADOXIDES
(LIKE A PUZZLE)

PRONOUNCED:
PAR-AH-DOX-E-DEES

GROUP: TRILOBITES

WHERE IT LIVED: CANADA,
EUROPE, NORTH AFRICA

WHEN IT LIVED: EARLY
TO MIDDLE CAMBRIAN
PERIOD (542 TO 513 MILLION
YEARS AGO)

LENGTH: 10 IN (25 CM)

SPECIAL FEATURES:
SPINES AT THE EDGE OF EACH
BODY SEGMENT

FOOD: PARTICLES ON THE
SEABED

MAIN ENEMY:
BIG ARTHROPODS

DID YOU KNOW?:
PARADOXIDES WAS ONE OF THE
FIRST TRILOBITES TO EVOLVE.

All trilobites had a big head shield, a tail shield, and a body with movable segments. Some could swim, some could burrow, and others could roll up into a ball.

Orthoceras

In the early Paleozoic Era, all animals lived in the ocean. *Orthoceras* was the biggest hunter of the time and could grow up to 3 feet (1 meter) long. It looked like an octopus housed in a long straight shell. Its strong tentacles were used to catch other animals.

The streamlined shell made it easy for *Orthoceras* to chase prey. By squirting water forward, it pushed itself backward in lightening-fast bursts.

Animal fact file

NAME: ORTHOCERAS
(STRAIGHT SHELL)

PRONOUNCED:
ORTH-OH-SEER-US

GROUP: CEPHALOPODS

WHERE IT LIVED: WORLDWIDE

WHEN IT LIVED: ORDOVICIAN
PERIOD (488 TO 444 MILLION
YEARS AGO)

LENGTH: 6 IN (15 CM)
TO 3 FT (1 M)

SPECIAL FEATURES: SHELL
WITH MANY CHAMBERS

FOOD: OTHER SEA ANIMALS

MAIN ENEMY: NONE

DID YOU KNOW?: ORTHOCERAS
FOSSILS ARE FAIRLY COMMON
AND OFTEN SOLD IN FOSSIL
SHOPS.

The shell had many chambers.
When they were full of air
Orthoceras could float. To sink
down it filled the
chambers with water.

Diplograptus

In the surface waters of early Paleozoic times lived strange creatures that looked like jellyfish. These were graptolite colonies. The *Diplograptus* were a type of graptolite. They had two rows of cups back to back. Each cup contained an animal. The cups were attached to a UFO-shaped unit called a float. Colonies drifted through the oceans anchored to their floats.

A graptolite colony looked like the blade of a saw. Each "tooth" was a tiny cup that held one animal. Dozens of individuals lived in a colony.

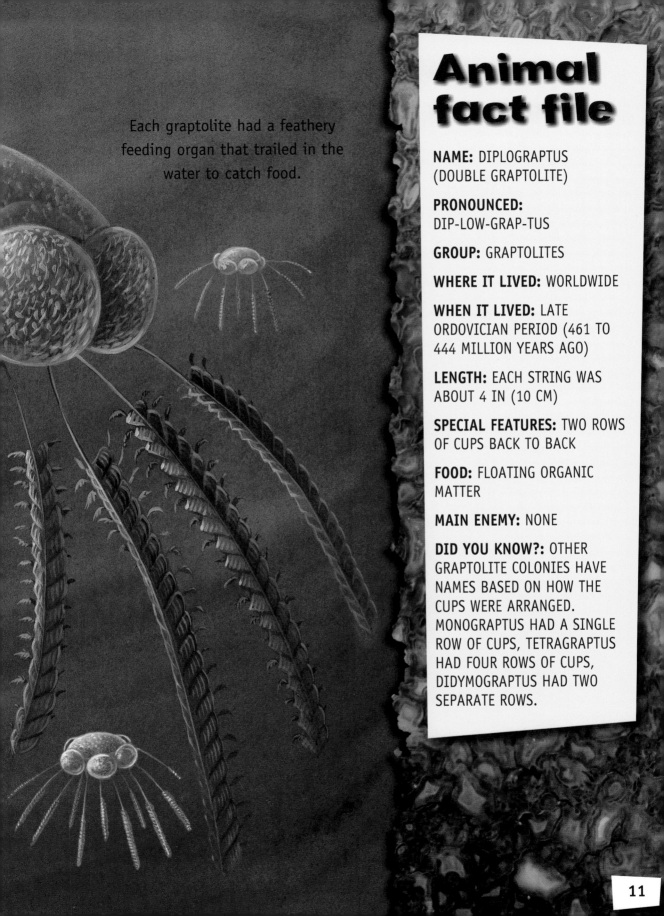

Each graptolite had a feathery feeding organ that trailed in the water to catch food.

Animal fact file

NAME: DIPLOGRAPTUS (DOUBLE GRAPTOLITE)

PRONOUNCED: DIP-LOW-GRAP-TUS

GROUP: GRAPTOLITES

WHERE IT LIVED: WORLDWIDE

WHEN IT LIVED: LATE ORDOVICIAN PERIOD (461 TO 444 MILLION YEARS AGO)

LENGTH: EACH STRING WAS ABOUT 4 IN (10 CM)

SPECIAL FEATURES: TWO ROWS OF CUPS BACK TO BACK

FOOD: FLOATING ORGANIC MATTER

MAIN ENEMY: NONE

DID YOU KNOW?: OTHER GRAPTOLITE COLONIES HAVE NAMES BASED ON HOW THE CUPS WERE ARRANGED. MONOGRAPTUS HAD A SINGLE ROW OF CUPS, TETRAGRAPTUS HAD FOUR ROWS OF CUPS, DIDYMOGRAPTUS HAD TWO SEPARATE ROWS.

Cephalaspis

Fish evolved early in the Paleozoic Era. Cephalaspis was one of the first to appear. Like all early fish, it had no jaws, just a sucker for a mouth. *Cephalaspis* did not have much of a skeleton either—only a backbone and a skull. Its head was protected by an armored shield.

Cephalaspis fed at the bottom of lakes and streams. The fin on its tail pushed the head downward, while the sucker mouth sifted through sand and mud for food.

These fossil fish were the earliest vertebrates—animals with backbones.

Dunkleosteus

The Devonian Period was the "Age of Fish." Many different kinds of fish lived in the ocean depths, the shallow seas, and in the world's rivers. Little fish lived on scraps of food, but some big fish were fierce hunters. *Dunkleosteus* was one of the biggest and fiercest.

Dunkleosteus belonged to a group of fish that had armored heads and necks. Its "teeth" were actually bone plates with razor-sharp edges. They could easily bite through flesh.

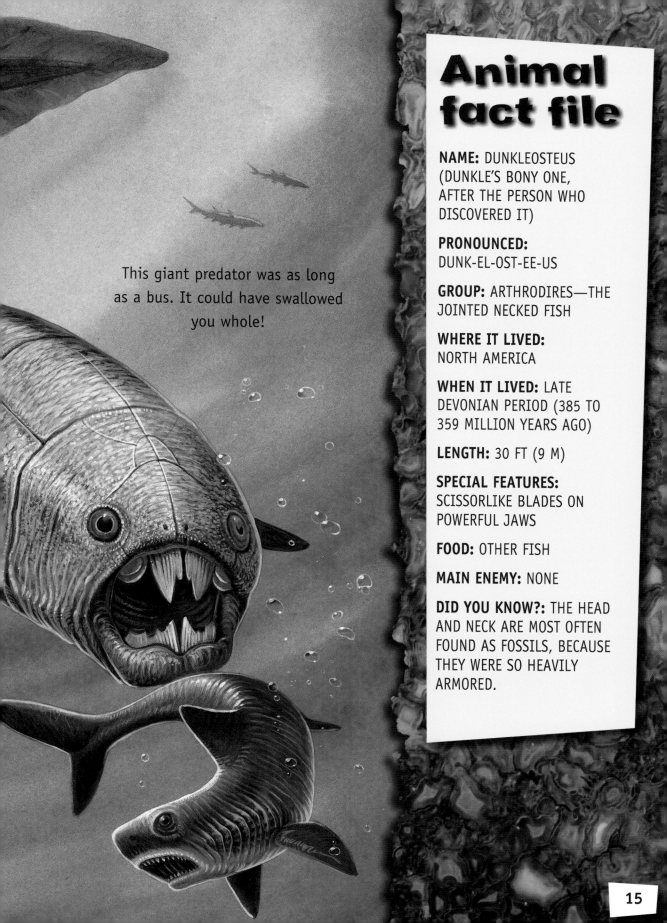

This giant predator was as long as a bus. It could have swallowed you whole!

Animal fact file

NAME: DUNKLEOSTEUS (DUNKLE'S BONY ONE, AFTER THE PERSON WHO DISCOVERED IT)

PRONOUNCED: DUNK-EL-OST-EE-US

GROUP: ARTHRODIRES—THE JOINTED NECKED FISH

WHERE IT LIVED: NORTH AMERICA

WHEN IT LIVED: LATE DEVONIAN PERIOD (385 TO 359 MILLION YEARS AGO)

LENGTH: 30 FT (9 M)

SPECIAL FEATURES: SCISSORLIKE BLADES ON POWERFUL JAWS

FOOD: OTHER FISH

MAIN ENEMY: NONE

DID YOU KNOW?: THE HEAD AND NECK ARE MOST OFTEN FOUND AS FOSSILS, BECAUSE THEY WERE SO HEAVILY ARMORED.

Tiktaalik

A few fish from the Devonian Period were able to spend time out of the water. *Tiktaalik* was one such fish. Half fish, half land animal, it had lungs and could breathe air. Although it only came on land for short periods, it was the first backboned animal to do so.

Tiktaalik lived in streams and ponds. When these dried up in hot weather it crawled over land to find a new watery home.

Bones inside the fins looked like elbows and wrists. The head resembled a crocodile's.

Animal fact file

NAME: TIKTAALIK (AN INUIT WORD FOR A BIG FISH)

PRONOUNCED: TIK-TA-LICK

GROUP: RHIPIDISTIANS—WITH FINS THAT COULD MOVE THEM ON LAND OR IN WATER

WHERE IT LIVED: NORTHERN CANADA

WHEN IT LIVED: LATE DEVONIAN PERIOD (375 MILLION YEARS AGO)

LENGTH: 9 FT (2.7 M)

SPECIAL FEATURES: TWO PAIRS OF FINS USED LIKE LEGS; LUNGS FOR BREATHING ON LAND

FOOD: SMALL FISH OR ARTHROPODS

MAIN ENEMY: BIGGER FISH

DID YOU KNOW?: THERE ARE FISH TODAY, SUCH AS THE MUDSKPPER, THAT SPEND TIME ON LAND.

Ichthyostega

Ichthyostega is the earliest known amphibian. Although it had the body, legs, and toes of a land-dwelling animal, it had the head of a fish and a fishlike fin on its tail. Clearly, its ancestors were fish.

Even though it could live on land, *Ichthyostega* probably spent most of its time in the water. It used its feet to push through thick water weeds.

Ichthyostega probably had a lifestyle similar to that of the mudskipper, which is found in tropical regions today. Mudskippers are fish, but they are adapted to life on land, too.

Animal fact file

NAME: ICHTHYOSTEGA (FISH SKULL)

PRONOUNCED: ICK-THEE-OH-STAY-GA

GROUP: LABYRINTHODONTS— THE EARLIEST AMPHIBIANS

WHERE IT LIVED: GREENLAND

WHEN IT LIVED: LATE DEVONIAN PERIOD (385 TO 359 MILLION YEARS AGO)

LENGTH: 3 FT (1 M)

SPECIAL FEATURES: STRONG SHOULDERS AND HIPS TO WORK THE LEGS AND FEET

FOOD: INSECTS AND OTHER SMALL ANIMALS

MAIN ENEMY: BIG FISH

DID YOU KNOW?: ICHTHYOSTEGA HAD STRANGE FEET. IT HAD EIGHT TOES ON ITS HIND FOOT AND SIX ON THE FRONT. LATER BACKBONED ANIMALS HAD A MAXIMUM OF FIVE TOES ON EACH FOOT.

Crassigyrinus

By the time of the Carboniferous Period, many amphibians were able to spend more time on land. However, some amphibians spent their lives completely in the water. *Crassigyrinus* was one of these.

Crassigyrinus had big eyes. They would have helped it see in the murky, weed-choked waters of the Carboniferous swamps.

Crassigyrinus was like a big eel (as above), swimming along with powerful swings of its huge tail. Its tiny front limbs acted as balancing fins.

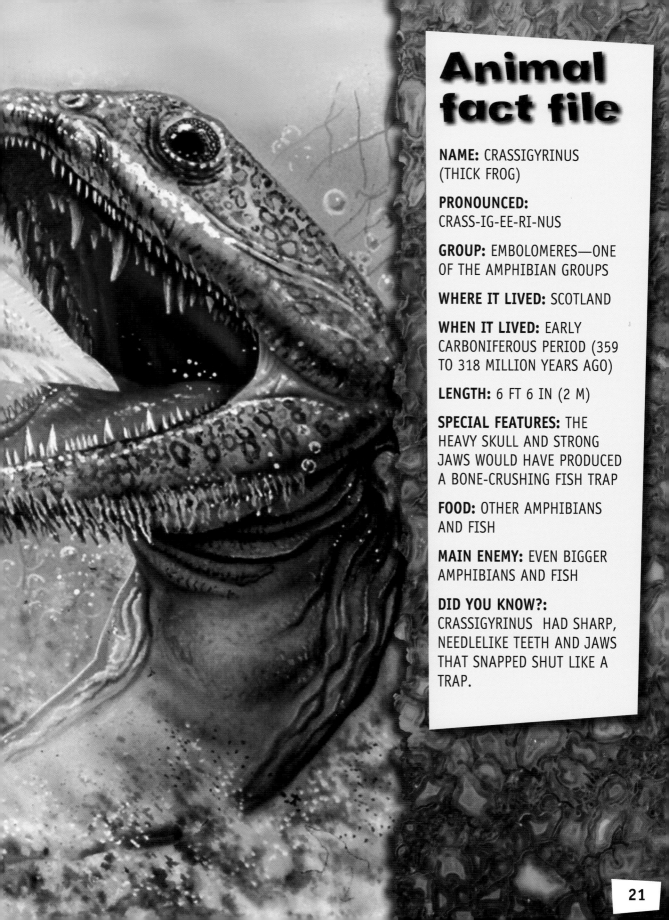

Animal fact file

NAME: CRASSIGYRINUS (THICK FROG)

PRONOUNCED: CRASS-IG-EE-RI-NUS

GROUP: EMBOLOMERES—ONE OF THE AMPHIBIAN GROUPS

WHERE IT LIVED: SCOTLAND

WHEN IT LIVED: EARLY CARBONIFEROUS PERIOD (359 TO 318 MILLION YEARS AGO)

LENGTH: 6 FT 6 IN (2 M)

SPECIAL FEATURES: THE HEAVY SKULL AND STRONG JAWS WOULD HAVE PRODUCED A BONE-CRUSHING FISH TRAP

FOOD: OTHER AMPHIBIANS AND FISH

MAIN ENEMY: EVEN BIGGER AMPHIBIANS AND FISH

DID YOU KNOW?: CRASSIGYRINUS HAD SHARP, NEEDLELIKE TEETH AND JAWS THAT SNAPPED SHUT LIKE A TRAP.

Westlothiana

One big difference between amphibians and reptiles is that reptiles lay their eggs on land, while amphibians lay their eggs in water. It is thought that *Westlothiana* could lay its eggs on land, making it the first reptile.

Westlothiana looked like a little lizard. It probably lived like one, too, chasing insects through the undergrowth.

Animal fact file

NAME: CAMPTOSAURUS (FLEXIBLE LIZARD)

PRONOUNCED: KAMP-TUH-SORE-US

GROUP: ORNITHOPOD DINOSAURS

WHERE IT LIVED: WESTERN UNITED STATES

WHEN IT LIVED: LATE JURASSIC PERIOD

LENGTH: 23 FEET (7 METERS)

FEATURES: SMALL HEAD, STRONG BEAK, GRINDING TEETH

FOOD: LOW-GROWING PLANTS

MAIN ENEMY: BIG MEAT-EATERS LIKE ALLOSAURUS

DID YOU KNOW?: SKELETONS OF CAMPTOSAURUS WERE FOUND IN THE 1880S.

The one *Westlothiana* fossil found so far was discovered in a quarry along with fossils of spiders, scorpions, and plants. They all lived in a swampy forest.

Dimetrodon

The Permian Period was the last period of the Paleozoic Era. When it began, deserts covered much of the Earth. *Dimetrodon* was a reptile that was well adapted to living in the hot, dry conditions.

On cold desert mornings *Dimetrodon* turned sideways to the sun and took in heat through its sail. In the heat of the day, wind passing over the sail cooled it down.

Dimetrodon had two types of teeth, which is unusual for a reptile. Long front teeth cut through meat, and short back ones tore it into small pieces.

Animal fact file

NAME: DIMETRODON (TWO KINDS OF TEETH)

PRONOUNCED: DI-MET-RO-DON

GROUP: PELYCOSAURS

WHERE IT LIVED: TEXAS

WHEN IT LIVED: EARLY PERMIAN PERIOD (299 TO 271 MILLION YEARS AGO)

LENGTH: 4 FT (3.3 M)

SPECIAL FEATURES: TALL SPINES COVERED BY SKIN, FORMING A SAIL ON ITS BACK

FOOD: OTHER REPTILES

MAIN ENEMY: NONE

DID YOU KNOW?: MANY PEOPLE WRONGLY THINK THAT DIMETRODON WAS A DINOSAUR. IT LIVED LONG BEFORE THE DINOSAURS AND WAS NOT RELATED AT ALL.

Lycaenops

Lycaenops had a long skull with sharp teeth and long legs that enabled it to run fast. Many scientists think it lived in packs and looked and behaved a lot like a wolf. Permian reptiles like Lycaenops are the distant ancestors of mammals.

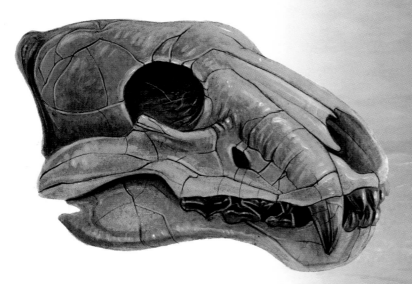

Lycaenops had killing teeth at the front of its mouth and meat-shredding teeth at the back. Modern wolves use their teeth in the same way.

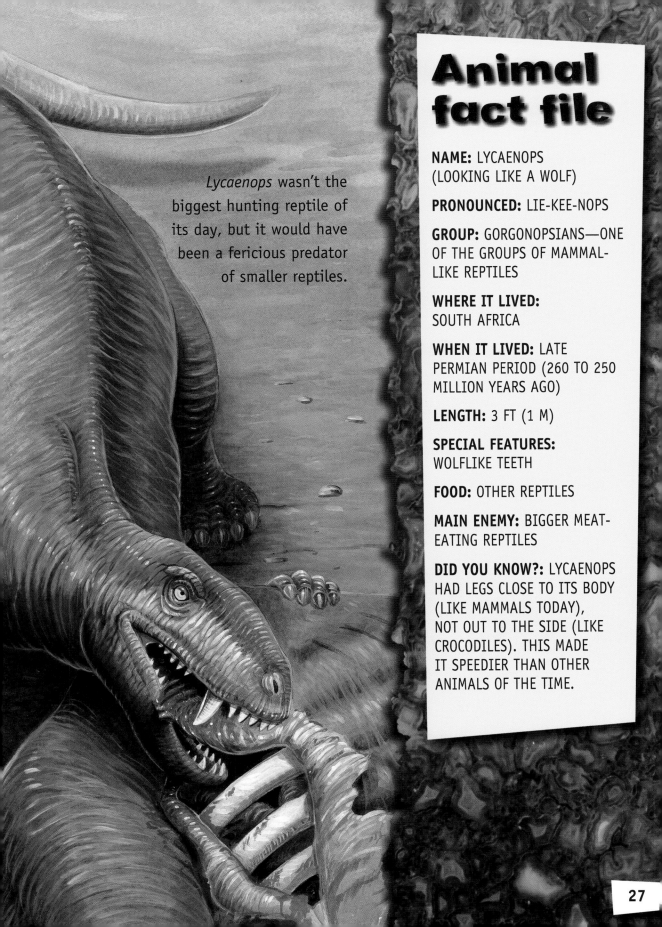

Lycaenops wasn't the biggest hunting reptile of its day, but it would have been a fericious predator of smaller reptiles.

Animal fact file

NAME: LYCAENOPS (LOOKING LIKE A WOLF)

PRONOUNCED: LIE-KEE-NOPS

GROUP: GORGONOPSIANS—ONE OF THE GROUPS OF MAMMAL-LIKE REPTILES

WHERE IT LIVED: SOUTH AFRICA

WHEN IT LIVED: LATE PERMIAN PERIOD (260 TO 250 MILLION YEARS AGO)

LENGTH: 3 FT (1 M)

SPECIAL FEATURES: WOLFLIKE TEETH

FOOD: OTHER REPTILES

MAIN ENEMY: BIGGER MEAT-EATING REPTILES

DID YOU KNOW?: LYCAENOPS HAD LEGS CLOSE TO ITS BODY (LIKE MAMMALS TODAY), NOT OUT TO THE SIDE (LIKE CROCODILES). THIS MADE IT SPEEDIER THAN OTHER ANIMALS OF THE TIME.

Estemmenosuchus

In the Permian Period, the climate was warm and the continents were joined in a giant landmass called Pangaea. Some regions had lakes and streams where plants grew. These areas were inhabited by plant-eating reptiles such as *Estemmenosuchus*, which was as big as a hippopotamus!

Estemmenosuchus probably lived in small herds, munching away on the fernlike plants and conifers that formed the main vegetation at the time.

Estemmenosuchus had strange horns on its head. These may have helped the animals identify one other, or they may have been used as weapons.

Animal fact file

NAME: ESTEMMENOSUCHUS (CROWNED CROCODILE)

PRONOUNCED: ES-TEM-EN-OH-SOOK-US

GROUP: DINOCEPHALIAS— A GROUP OF THE MAMMAL-LIKE REPTILES

WHERE IT LIVED: EASTERN RUSSIA

WHEN IT LIVED: THE LATE PERMIAN PERIOD (260 TO 250 MILLION YEARS AGO)

LENGTH: 13 FT (4 M)

SPECIAL FEATURES: HORNS AROUND THE HEAD

FOOD: PLANTS

MAIN ENEMY: GORGONOPSIANS SUCH AS LYCAENOPS AND ITS RELATIVES

DID YOU KNOW?: EVEN THOUGH ESTEMMENOSUCHUS LOOKED FIERCE AND HAD BIG TEETH, IT WAS A PLANT-EATER.

Animal Families Glossary

Agnathas—the most primitive fish type. They lacked jaws and had a sucker for a mouth, like the modern lamprey, and lived mostly in Silurian and Devonian times.

Arthrodires—a primitive group of fish with armored heads and necks. The name means "jointed neck" and refers to the arrangement of armor. They were the terror of Devonian seas.

Arthropods—invertebrates with an outside shell and jointed legs. They include modern insects, crabs, and spiders. The shell is made of material like fingernails.

Cephalopods—literally the "head-footed" animals. The modern types, the octopus and squid, seem to have legs branching from their faces. In prehistoric times many of them had chambered shells.

Rhipidistians—the fish that could spend some time on land. They had lungs and muscular fins and gave rise to the amphibians.

Dicynodonts—the group of mammal-like reptiles that had a pair of teeth at the front that looked like those of a wolf. They were mostly plant-eaters.

Embolomeres—a group of Carboniferous amphibians with very long bodies that swam by twisting like eels.

Gorgonopsians—a fierce group of mammal-like reptiles that looked like a cross between a crocodile and a saber-toothed tiger. They lived mainly in late Permian times.

Graptolites—a group of tiny sea-dwelling animals that consisted of a string of individuals attached to a stalk. They floated in the waters of the Silurian seas.

Labyrinthodonts—one of the groups of early amphibians, from the Carboniferous and Permian Periods. They were so-called because the enamel of their teeth was contorted like a labyrinth, or maze.

Pelycosaurs—the most primitive group of the mammal-like reptiles, from early Permian times. Most of them had big fins on their backs. Some were meat-eaters and others were plant-eaters.

Trilobites—a group of common sea-dwelling arthropods, common from Cambrian to Devonian times. They had head shields, tail shields, and a body divided into segments in between.

Glossary

Adapted—changing to survive in a particular habitat or weather conditions.

Amphibian—an animal that is able to live on both land and in the water.

Ancestor—an early form of the animal group that lived in the past.

Cold-blooded—animals, such as reptiles or amphibians, that rely on their environment to control their body temperature.

Colony—a group of animals of the same kind living closely together.

Conifer—an evergreen tree such as a pine.

Continent—one of the world's main landmasses such as Africa and Europe.

Dinosaur—a large group of meat-eating or plant-eating reptiles that no longer exist.

Evolution—changes or developments that happen to all life-forms over millions of years, as a result of changes in the environment.

Evolve—to change or develop through time.

Fossil—the remains of a prehistoric plant or animal that has been buried for a long time and become hardened in rock.

Fossilized—turned into a fossil.

Mammal—a warm-blooded animal that is covered in hair. The female gives birth to live young and produces milk to feed them.

Meat-shearing teeth—special teeth that are used to cut or slice the flesh from bones.

Organic matter—really tiny animal or plant life.

Paleozoic Era—the period when life first appeared on Earth.

Predator—an animal that hunts and kills other animals for food.

Prehistory—a time before humans evolved.

Prey—animals that are hunted by other animals as food.

Primitive—a very early stage in the development of a group of plants or animals.

Reptile—a cold-blooded, crawling or creeping animal with a backbone.

Segmented—divided into separate parts.

Sift—to separate food from water when feeding.

Species—a group of animals that all share similar traits.

Tropic—a region of hot countries that is close to the equator.

Index

Picture credits

Main illustrations: 8-9, 12-13, 24-25 Simon Mendez; 6-7, 20-21, 28-29 Luis Rey;
10-11, 14-15, 16-17, 18-19, 22-23, 26-27 Chris Tomlin 4 TL, 4TR, 5 (Cenozoic Era),
6, 9, 10, 13, 14, 17 Ticktock Media archive; 5 (Mesozoic Era top, Paleozoic Era top),
23 Simon Mendez; 5 (Mesozoic Era centre, Paleozoic Era bottom) Luis Rey; 5 (Mesozoic
Era bottom) Lisa Alderson; 18 Hu Lan /Alamy; 20 Shutterstock; 25 Mervyn Rees/
Alamy; 26 Chris Tomlin; 28 Gondwana Studios